Steady Along

By James Michael Orr

Steady Along

Copyright 2021 By James Michael Orr

All Rights Reserved. This book or any portion therof may not be reproduced or used in any manner whatsoever without the express written permission of the publisher except for the use of brief quotations in a book review.

First Edition, 2021

ISBN# 978-1-7357518-1-8

Cover Art: Joy Orr

Editing: Mariko Irving

EireneBros Publishing LLC

4414 82nd St, Ste 212, -318

Lubbock, TX 79424

www.eirenebros.com

www.facebook.com/EireneBrosPublishing

To my beautiful wife, who inspires me every day.

To my friend Stephanie, the inspiration behind many of these poems.

To Jillian, Joy, Joshua, and Jaycee, the children I always wished for.

To the team at EireneBros for giving me a shot

To Christ, who is my Alpha and Omega

Forward

There are times when I look at my life as if I were in a boat floating along a long and winding river. In this scenario, there would be times when the river would rush forward and other times where it seemed as if everything stood still.

The success of such a journey would not depend on the river or the speed of the river. Instead, it would be the boat itself and the course that was taken. I imagine a course in life determined by God and a boat built on faith in Jesus. All other courses and all other boats would lead to disaster. This book was written with a simple message in that vein: Take the path that God has provided and put your faith in Christ alone. He is the boat that takes us forward and leads us to the end of the river's course. As the poem that inspired this book repeatedly says, "steady along" is the way home for those who trust in Jesus.

Many of these poems were written for a dear friend of mine who I wanted to encourage during a time in her life when she was looking for answers. She helped inspire many of the poems you read. An entire section is dedicated to many people I lost during the pandemic and still wish to honor after leaving this world.

My hope is that as you read through these poems, you will get a sense of how faith takes us through the course of life, steady and ever onward, if we will but trust in the One who urges us forward. May God be with you as you read these thoughts of mine and bless you with a good and successful year.

Table of Contents

Section One - Faith   6
- Steady Along   7
- He Waits for Me   9
- Rejoicing on this Day   10
- There is Beauty in You   12
- Step Up to the Plate   13
- I'll Stand with You   14
- Father, Forgive Them   15
- What Does Beautiful Look Like?   17
- The Way We Spend It   18
- You Follow Me   19
- If I Had Enough Time   21
- Love Unending   23
- Just as You Made Me   24
- River Longing   25
- Righteous Living   27
- What Do You Want, Jesus?   28
- The Love of Christ   30
- When God's in Control   31
- I Finally See   32
- In the Presence of the Lord   33

Section Two – Nature   34
- Every Moment   35
- If You Ever   37
- Those That Bloom   38
- I Didn't Like   39
- In One Day   41
- Walking in the Light   43
- The Little Branch   45
- The Morning After   47

The Colors of the Sky	48
The Dawn is There	49
Perfect Light	50
The Stinging Cold	51
The Sun Sets Far Too Quickly	53
In the Dawning of the Day	55
A Light that Follows Me	56

Section Three – Loss   **57**

Forever in Our Hearts	58
I Know You're Still with Me	60
I Thought I Saw	62
My Dearest Friend	63
When I'm Thinking Back on You	65
Tears Aren't Forever	67
Eternity Calls	68

Section Four – Inspiration   **69**

A Little Dream	70
Everything and Anything	72
I Tripped and Fell	74
In Your Smile	75
Life Makes a Window	76
Lonely Street Lamp	77
More Beautiful	78
Reflection	79
The Choice	81
How Do You Sing?	82
No One Stopped Me	84

Section One: Faith

Growing up faith was always a big part of my life. My father is an evangelist and preached at many congregations throughout my childhood. Wherever we were, Church and God were a daily part of our lives. I decided in the third grade to be a minister, and I stuck with that vision until I became one. Faith is life to those who choose to believe that life is not about our day-to-day circumstances but about the journey towards Heaven. The poems in this section are my bread and butter, written for matters that have to do with a faithful follower of Jesus Christ. I hope you enjoy them.

Steady Along

I find myself in a simple boat in waters unforgiving,
For my Lord and I were out to sea on the voyage, I call living,
I questioned if the boat was safe, for it seemed to be unsteady,
And he gave an answer to my doubts for which I wasn't ready,

"Steady along, for I am here, and you will never fail,
Steady along, for I am near, go forward and set sail."

Now holes appeared within the boat, and I was not amused,
And when I asked my Lord for help, He patiently refused,
He told me I must trust in him, and all would be made right,
But more kept springing all around in the thickness of the night,

I looked around to see if there was land that I could swim to,
In case I could not figure out the mess that I was into,
"Lord, please, the water rises now, and we must go ashore!"
I cried to him, yet he answered just the way He did before,

"Steady along, for I am here, and you will never fail,
Steady along, for I am near, go forward and set sail."

In panic, I jumped in the sea and swam with all my might,
Yet everywhere I looked, there wasn't any land in sight,
The waves grew strong and threw me hard until I lost my breath,
And as I fought, I felt on me the icy hand of death,

Now with my final effort, I called out to Him again,

Restoring all my faith that I had buried in my sin,
"Save me, Lord!" I cried to Him with heart and soul complete,
And Jesus walked up next to me upon the water's seat.

He lifted me out of the waves and led me to my ship,
The boat restored, as good as new, and ready for our trip,
The holes were gone that I had made with all my doubts defeated,
And then He looked to me again and lovingly repeated,

"Steady along, for I am here, and you will never fail,
Steady along, for I am near, go forward and set sail."

He Waits for Me

He waits for me,
in the quiet of the morning,
When none are yet risen,
Calling out my name again and again.

He waits for me,
In the stillness of the evening,
When all are retiring,
Looking for my form in the twilight.

He waits for me,
Yearning for me to come back,
Wishing for yesterday's laughter,
Longing for tomorrow's rejoicing.

He waits for me,
An empty seat at the table,
A room untouched since I left,
A host of angels hoping for my return.

He waits for me,
Door still open,
Feast at the ready,
Arms open for a welcome…

He waits for me to come home.

Rejoicing on this Day

We saw you in the Word, said the prophets from the past,
Virgin born and God in flesh, eternal, first and last,
Your coming was expected, though many turned away,
Yet those who sought your coming are rejoicing on this day.

We saw you in a manger, said the shepherds who had heard,
The angels sang their chorus and were true unto their word,
For in this humble city, we have seen the living Way,
And now we spread the news to all rejoicing on this day.

We saw you in the star, said the wise men from the east,
The signs were not forgotten, not even in the least,
We bring you gifts abundant, but no riches could repay,
The hope that you have brought us, rejoicing on this day.

We saw you in the temple, said the teachers gathered there,
Your questions were amazing; nothing to them could compare,
We'd never guess the reason for the things you found to say,
For if we knew we'd all be found rejoicing on this day.

We saw you heal the masses, said the twelve you singled out,
To follow you and learn from you, there wasn't any doubt,
That you are Christ, the chosen one, each one of us will stay,
And see this work until the end, rejoicing on this day.

We saw you on the cross, said the women at the tomb,
For all you called apostles fled within the upper room,
Our hearts completely broken, our future dark and gray,
But little did we know we'd be rejoicing on this day.

We saw you resurrected, five hundred people said,

Our Lord and Savior came to us, now risen from the dead,
Let all the weak and weary, now turn to Him and pray,
That Christ would come and take us home, rejoicing on this day.

There is Beauty in You

There is beauty in you, soul-deep in high definition,
Beauty in you, crystal clear and without condition,
Beauty in you, pristine and shielded from all degradation,
Beauty in you, far beyond any cheap imitation,

There is beauty in you, forged with grace and perfection,
Beauty in you, flawless on the closest inspection,
Beauty in you, brilliant with hues iridescent,
Beauty in you, teeming with depth near incessant.

There is beauty in you, holding strong, fast and steady,
Beauty in you, with your heart at the ready,
Beauty in you, in your visage, revealed,
Beauty in you, in your smile, unsealed.

There is beauty in you, shining brightly before you,
Beauty in you, those who see will adore you,
Beauty in you makes a dark place seem brighter,
Beauty in you makes the twilight seem lighter.

There is beauty in you, formed with eternal intention,
Beauty in you, in divine intervention,
Beauty in you, by the maker's demand,
Beauty in you, in the palm of His hand.

Step Up to the Plate

The crowd is in the bleachers; they're watching what you'll do,
The team is in the dugout; they're cheering just for you,
The other team is fielded, there's no more time to wait,
For your bat is at the ready, so step up to the plate.

No one can do it for you, no one can take your place,
The challenge you've been given is yours alone to face,
You don't know what is coming, but it won't be coming late,
For your moment is arriving, so step up to the plate.

Now life will throw a change-up, a fastball or a curve,
So, you must be at the ready, and all your strength reserve,
In your feet, you hold position; in your hands, you hold your fate,
For you know the ball is coming, so step up to the plate,

There are souls that are in danger, there are hearts devoid of love,
There's a battle all around you, here below and up above,
It's no time for distraction when you stand at Heaven's gate,
For the day is fast approaching, so step up to the plate.

Now swing with all your courage, connect with all your might,
For you're sure to hit a homer when you're walking in the light,
Renew your strength and purpose, let go of every weight,
For the time is now upon you, so step up to the plate.

I'll Stand with You

I'll stand with you, when you're all alone,
When the future and present, are all an unknown,
In the trials you're facing, in the things that you do,
I'll be right here waiting, to stand there with you.

I'll stand with you, when your tears are free flowing,
When the sorrow you carry, is steadily growing,
In the wake of your grieving, from old pain or new,
I'll be here every moment, to stand there with you.

I'll stand with you, when your faith has been tested,
When hardship is certain, and your all is invested.
Regardless of outcome, or the things you've been through,
I'm here at the ready, to stand there with you.

I'll stand with you, in life and in living,
For the fortune of friendship, is found in the giving,
And when we reach glory, in Eternity's view,
I'll rejoice in that moment, to stand there with you.

Father, Forgive Them

Father, forgive them...
But what about the shameless crowd whose views I find disgusting?
Don't you think your simple plea might need some readjusting?
Forgive, He said, for broken lives retain a wounded soul,
And they all need my Father's love to make them truly whole.

Father, forgive them...
But what about the howling mob whose evil deeds betray you?
Or all the fake pretenders who are trying now to play you?
Forgive, He said, for sin is sin and all have fallen short,
They need to know of saving grace, not cynical retort.

Father, forgive them...
But what about the leaders who did nothing but berate?
Whose jealous thoughts and wicked lies led everyone to hate?
Forgive, He said, for though they failed, they're blindly sinning too,
And though their sin is evident, they don't know what they do.

Father, forgive them...
But what about the person who has wronged me to the core?'
Or those whom I've forgiven once, and now they hurt me more?
Forgive, He said, for if you don't, your heart cannot be right,
For all who cling to bitterness rejects The Father's light.

Father, forgive me...
For I have judged my fellow man, my angry thoughts reserving,
When grace has washed my filthy soul when I was undeserving,
Forgiven, Jesus said to me, for that is why I died,
To free the soul from guilt of sin, so with them, I'd abide.

Forgive them now with softened heart so you will truly see,
That they and you are just the same, for all, I died to free.

What Does Beautiful Look Like?

What does beautiful look like?
A kind smile and a loving embrace,
Eyes of compassion on a friendly face,
Hands that serve and a shoulder to cry on,
And a look reassuring you can always rely on.

What does successful look like?
A life that brings honor to father and mother,
Takes to heart the command to love one another,
A soul that cries out as deep calls to deep,
A mind that is faithful and a promise to keep.

What does powerful look like?
Lips filled with wisdom that comes from above,
A tongue that speaks only in truth and in love,
A voice that resounds with God-centered glory,
A mouth that can't help but tell others the Story.

What does faithful look like?
A head bowed in prayer and continued devotion,
Feet that walk straight in continuous motion,
Shoulders that carry the burden of all,
And a life at the ready to answer His call.

The Way We Spend It

Everyone has power and strength to use,
Distributed as needed however they choose,
Vitality spent on work or for pleasure,
Displaying in full the things they most treasure,
But try as we might to hide or defend it,
Our measure of worth is found where we spend it.

On joy or on sorrow, on bitter or sweet,
On reveling in victory or lost in defeat,
The time and the passing are always the same,
We choose how we use it; no one else is to blame,
And regardless of why or how much we intend it,
The result is decided by how we spend it.

Perhaps we will choose to better our choices,
To drown out the chorus of self-serving voices,
Or live for the moment to nurture our greed,
And turn a blind eye to the stranger in need,
When time is unraveled, no power can mend it,
Our life will be judged in the manner we spend it.

For who is the author, and where is the pen?
Is it not written down in the choices of men?
We're given a moment to live in the sun,
And we're judged by the Maker for all that we've done,
When the writing is finished, we cannot rescind it,
We will all give account for the way that we spend it.

You Follow Me

You follow me,
Into the darkest depths of my inner being,
To the ugliest places far beyond seeing,
And you come as I'm wallowing in my deep-seated shame,
To cleanse me and wash me and give me your name.

You follow me,
Into my sin-weary mind,
Where my fears make me powerless, desperate, and blind,
And you come as I'm drained from my worries and doubt,
To transform my thinking both inside and out.

You follow me,
Into my heart filled with pain,
Inflicted by self from my sins done in vain,
And you come as I'm broken, feeble, and frail,
To strengthen my spirit and help me prevail.

You follow me,
Into my life's fleeting breath,
As I dwell in the lengthening shadow of death,
And you come as I'm spent on life's many pains,
To lead me to true life where eternity reigns.

You follow me,
But Lord, am I following you?
Am I faithful in all that I say, and I do?
Do I go where you want me, to the lost and in need?
Do I follow your will in truth and in deed?

You follow me,
You are with me, I know deep within,

Lord cleanse me and heal me from all my sin,
And may I follow with every step showing,
I know whom I serve, and I know where I'm going.

If I Had Enough Time

If I had enough time,
I'd write every song about love,
Of joy and sorrow and pain,
Of mysteries below and above,
Of sunshine, of cloud, and of rain,

But I only have this moment…

If I had enough time,
I'd go to a thousand places,
I'd chase every dream I can dream,
I'd look on a billion new faces,
I'd make the world bright 'til it gleams,

But I only have this moment…

If I had enough time,
I'd try every food I am craving,
I'd play every game I find fun,
I'd dwell in the moments I'm saving,
I'd just do it all, every one,

But I only have this moment…

If I had enough time,
I'd visit the people I miss,
I'd finish the tasks uncompleted,
I'd linger in every long kiss,
I'd go through this life undefeated,

But I only have this moment…
So…

I'll give every moment its glory,
Every road that I take on the way,
Let God write the rest of my story,
And live to the fullest each day.

Love Unending

The words were softly spoken,
Gentle and assuring,
Listen to the promise,
Of sacred truth enduring.

Far beyond the ages,
Mystery still unfolding,
Love that knows no ending,
Your eyes are now beholding.

Spark of life and living,
Perfect and anointed,
Came with a single purpose,
For which He was appointed.

Sorrow and betrayal,
Pain and loss unyielding,
Love unending conquered,
For the world's rebuilding.

Raised in brightness shining,
Taken up in glory,
All for mercy's pardon,
Love's enduring story.

Spirit's calm assurance,
Until the call supernal,
Love without an ending,
Life that is eternal.

Just as You Made Me

I wish I were smarter, I said in my brain,
So I'd prosper in all that we do, I explain,
If you wouldn't shut down when you're tired from use,
We'd be able to table your feeble excuse.

I wish I were stronger, I said to my body,
So we'd look more attractive, and never so shoddy,
If you'd only try a bit more when you're tired,
And perform at your best when your best is required.

I wish I were tougher, I said to my heart,
So we wouldn't be sad when love must depart,
If you'd stop letting sorrow and pain interfere,
I could brush off the heartbreak and dry every tear.

I wish I were cleaner, I said to my soul,
So we'd feel much more worthy and perfectly whole,
If you'd work hard enough, I am sure you'll do better,
And pay every cost that you owe to your debtor,

You're just as I made you, said the Father to me,
So heart, mind, and body, would rely upon me,
And your soul will be clean when you follow my will,
So the scars in your being can recover and heal.

I'm just as you made me, I respond as I pray,
That I would accept who I am every day,
A servant, a child, beloved and new,
For all that I am was created by You.

River Longing

How I long for streams of running water,
A fitting home for fish and otter,
Trickling down its rugged bed,
The promise of new life ahead.

For in the river's ebb and flow,
Therein abides more than we know,
A symbol of the life above,
Of purest stream and perfect love.

In my mind's eye, I'm drawing near,
To gaze on waters crystal clear,
A river flows from Holy Throne,
In places far and yet unknown.

Within the river stands a tree,
Eternal life, how can it be?
The leaves for healing, fruit for living,
Every day new life it's giving.

Tree and water for the curse,
As sin and death will now reverse,
The river runs to bring together,
Every soul in Christ forever.

Now I yearn to run and find,
The place where rivers bend and wind,
Reminding me of Holy visions,
Flowing through my life's decisions.

So come and sit beside the river,
Peace and calm it will deliver,

Flowing stream and soothing foam,
Reminding us we'll soon be home.

Righteous Living

Come and dwell in lovingkindness,
Where the fields are full of grace,
Where light replaces blindness,
With a smile upon each face.

Come and live on love and blessing,
In a home where God is present,
And in every window dressing,
You see all things good and pleasant.

Come and share God's great ambition,
With the saints in mind and glory,
Where the soul's redeemed condition,
Is a witness to our story.

Come and turn away from sinning,
And refrain your tongue from lying,
For the battle, we are winning,
When to wickedness, we're dying.

Come and take of grace upon us,
In your prayers that you are giving,
For His eyes and ears are on us,
When in righteousness, we're living.

What Do You Want, Jesus?

What do you want from me, Jesus? I don't have a clue.
This week I spent FOUR HOURS worshipping you!
Every day I study for ten minutes or so,
Pray three times a day when I remember, you know.

But really, what more do you want, Jesus?
Why don't you just say?
Do I need to start helping a stranger each day?
Maybe I can give a bit more in the plate,
I guess that next upgrade on my house can just wait.

So, what else do you want, Jesus? Am I doing enough?
Perhaps I can learn to stop caring about stuff,
Invest more in people, watch less on TV,
And stop being so focused on what's in it for me.

Now tell me, Lord Jesus, how to follow your will,
I'll check every box that you give me to fill,
Each commandment I'll keep with gladness and joy,
I'll be the best Christian you'll ever employ.

And then...Jesus answered.

What do I want from you, my little one, you say?
I want you to love me in every small way,
Love your neighbor, enemies, and friends in your heart,
But love me the most, yes, that's where I'd start.

What do I want from you? Well, It's simple, my friend,
I want all this conflict and striving to end,
You can never earn back what I did out of love,
Or work your way into a home up above.

What I want from you…Simple, trust only in me,
Let me take all your burdens…I'll do it for free!
Ask all that you need, and I'll help you in kind,
I'll pour out every blessing; I really don't mind.

What do I want from you? Easy. What I already own:
Your life and your body, down to every small bone,
So I can fill you with fullness, my love, and my grace,
Shine my light in your being, in every dark place.

So you ask what I want, well I'll tell you, it's true,
Eternally, thoroughly, I only want you.

The Love of Christ

It's in the kindness to souls in need,
It's in the hungry we help to feed,
It's in the comfort to those who mourn,
It's in the hope to those forlorn.

It's in the loss of bitter pride,
It's in the healing when hearts divide,
It's in the fences we have mended,
It's in the grace when we're offended.

It's in the love without conditions,
It's in the heart with pure intentions,
It's in the hand that holds no wrath,
It's in the smooth and peaceful path.

It's in the soul that knows its Maker,
It's in the giver, not the taker,
It's in the gentle filled with meekness,
It's in the strength found in our weakness.

It's in the echoes of His grace,
It's in the look upon His face,
It's in the mercy on His throne,
It's in the love of Christ alone.

When God's in Control

If peace were an egg that was easily broken,
By a struggle or trial or word that was spoken,
It wouldn't be peace, for the peace I possess,
Is unbreakable, unshakeable, under any duress.

If hope were a feather that floated away,
With a gale of uncertainty on a dark, windy day,
It wouldn't be hope, for my hope is a tether,
To a tree firmly planted in life's stormy weather.

If love were a flower that died overnight,
When the cold of indifference deflected the light,
It wouldn't be love, for the love I've beheld,
Cannot be deflated, destroyed, or derailed.

If faith were a candle that melted and waned,
As it burned out with doubt so that nothing remained,
It wouldn't be faith, for my faith is a flame,
Ignited by trust that I place in His name.

For in peace and in hope, in faith and in love,
I look to the Lord and His Spirit above,
So if darkness abounds and troubles my soul,
I have all that I need when God's in control.

I Finally See

No longer will I sit upon the dais where you place me,
Judging value, worth in outward view where you all face me,
No longer will I let you tell me who I ought to be,
For all I am is clear and plain; at last, I finally see.

No longer will I play the games of who cares more or less,
For who thinks I am anything is anybody's guess,
The only one I truly need is always here with me,
For God's the one who loves me most, at last, I finally see.

No longer will I sacrifice to make the others need me,
Or think that their attention is enough to always feed me,
For I was but a sinner lost when Christ died on a tree,
His all is more than I could ask, at last, I finally see.

And now I die unto the world for it cannot compare,
To all the things I have in Him, I can't get anywhere,
And I will dream of things above so vast beyond degree,
For I am His, and He is mine, at last, I finally see.

In the Presence of the Lord

There is beauty in your footsteps,
Drops of glory in your ways,
Priceless treasures shine upon you,
In the counting of your days.

Mind of brilliance in the making,
Heart renewed, refreshed, restored,
For you stand in robes of glory,
In the presence of the Lord.

There is power in your being,
Healing waters flood your soul,
Countless blessings dress your Spirit,
Makes you full and truly whole.

On your head, you wear salvation,
Shield of faith and Spirit's sword,
For you fight and win each battle,
In the presence of the Lord.

There is joy within your speaking,
Perfect peace upon your face,
Shining hope rests on your shoulders,
Seamless love in your embrace.

Eyes of promise shine within you,
Hands are filled with your reward,
For you stand within the fullness
Of the presence of the Lord.

Section Two: Nature

Nature is everywhere. It is all around us in various forms, from the untouched majesty of God to the materials in all we choose to build and create. God's creation is simply unparalleled to anything man can achieve. Yet, we often take for granted the inherent beauty even in the parts we consider smaller or less impressive. To see not only nature but God's design behind it is to look upon the character and qualities of God. It is in His creation we see the intention He had when creating all that is around us. The poems in this section are dedicated to the beauty all around us, and as I wrote many of these while taking walks in my local park, it is fitting that all that I looked upon each day would inspire this humble creation to attempt the impossible…To put into words the greatness and glory of God's beautiful works.

Every Moment

The summer sky rushes before me,
I give chase as I run just to match it,
And the fall slips like rain through my fingers,
For I don't have the wisdom to catch it.

The winter snow melts in my viewing,
I don't ever take time to play in it,
And the Spring blooms and withers in moments,
Just as I find a day to begin it.

As days become years, I still wonder,
Will I ever just stop and reflect,
On the changing of moments and seasons,
That my crazy life seems to neglect?

If I stopped and just noticed the summer,
Caught the sun and just held it a bit,
Or felt the fall leaves in my footsteps,
Caught the rain in my hands just a bit.

If I took time to build me a snowman,
Let the winter cold into my door,
Watch the bee take in Spring from a rosebud,
Like I've never observed it before…

Would the years seem to last a bit longer,
If I held them as treasures each season?
Would I drink fuller, deeper than shallow,
If I lived every day for a reason?

So I'll shine with the sun every summer,
I'll catch every leaf in the fall,

And in Winter and Spring, I will linger,
And give every moment my all.

If You Ever

If you ever see a mountain reaching high up in the air,
If you ever see a river rush into a sea somewhere,
If you ever look upon a rose and wonder how it's growing,
If you ever look at migrant birds and ask them where they're going...

If you ever see a rainbow and you find the place it ends
If you ever see a falling star and watch as it descends
If you ever look upon a cloud and see a shape so clearly,
If you ever look into the moon and hold its gaze so dearly...

If you ever see the leaves that ride the rushing wind upon them,
If you ever see through pouring rain to the storm that's just beyond them,
If you ever look at your reflection through a still, calm lake,
If you ever look at every shape in every small snowflake...

If you ever see a baby's smile and feel your awe resounding,
If you ever see a lover's sigh and hear their heart a-pounding,
If you ever look upon a saint that hears their Savior's call,
If you ever look with teary eyes as you give to Christ your all...

If you ever see this wondrous sight,
Thank God for bringing these to light.

Those That Bloom

Those that bloom are not denied,
When ground is dry and sunbeams hide,
Nor do they let the bitter cold,
Destroy the bloom within the mold.

For those that bloom will never shrink,
When scorching sun dries to the brink,
Since the day of trouble cannot break,
The path the flower plans to take.

Those that bloom will flourish strong,
When days are short and nights are long,
No climate, nor its circumstance,
Can halt the flower's strong advance.

For those that bloom there is no stop,
In warmest heat or coldest drop,
Since those that bloom trust in the One
That plants the seed and made the sun.

I Didn't Like...

I didn't like the rain you sent; it made my day so dismal,
And now when I look to the sky, the world seems so abysmal,
Lord, if you'd send more sunny days, I'd be so glad, you see,
For the storms you sent are too intense, too difficult for me.

It was for you I sent the rain, the Lord replied in kind,
You needed dark and dismal days to clear your clouded mind,
For now, you're forced to look within and face the truth you're hiding,
That all the storms that threaten you have been in you residing.

I didn't like the sun today; it was too hot and searing,
For the light takes shadow from my heart, and that's what I've been fearing,
The happy days and blissful thoughts seem too good to be true,
And manifests my weariness in all I see and do.

It was for you I sent the sun, to clear away the lies,
And purify hypocrisy you know we both despise,
For brighter days won't mean a thing if you deny what's right,
For darkness hides the joy in you when you block out all the light.

I didn't like the cold today; it chilled me to the bone,
It isolated me within and made me feel alone,
If only you could make the weather perfect every season,
The things you send into my life would not seem so uneven.

It was for you I sent the cold, to make you seek my shelter,
To find the warmth you need from me, your one and only helper,
For warmth or cold or rain or shine, within you'll be okay,
If you decide to come to Me, and in my presence stay.

Oh, Lord, I thank you for the day, no matter what it brings,
And now, in times both bright and dark, my heart within me sings,
Though all the world seems out of place, my eyes can clearly see,
That rain or shine, if you are mine, it's wonderful to me.

In One Day

In one day, we see the sun creep above the sky in purple hue,
View reflection on each blade of grass within the morning dew,
Feel the cool air rush reminding us of the respite God brings in,
Watch a canopy of motion unfold as we see the day begin.

In one day, we hear the birds chirping their God-given symphony of sound,
Watch the trees rustling in the wind as the leaves take flight all around,
Smell the sweetness of a flower nestled in a garden glowing,
Consider the wonder of seeds turn to buds in the soil where they're growing,

In one day, we hear hundreds of thousands of babies take their first breath in life,
Witness two hundred thousand people make a pledge to be husband and wife,
Marvel, as billions of souls all around the world, work and laugh and play,
Wonder how all of it is accomplished in the span of a single, most ordinary day.

In one day, we witness the sunset upon orange hues of brilliant light,
Gaze at innumerable stars casting twinkling spotlights on the night,
Listen to the crickets play a steady violin of sound as their motion keeps their time,
Search for the lighting bugs shining above the meadow in a setting most sublime.

In one day, we observe our creator move the heavens and earth once more,
Look in awe as He rotates our spinning globe just as he's done countless times before,
And ask if we could but stop to give him glory in the things we do and say,
Imagine if we could begin to fathom all He's done for us in just one day.

Walking in the Light

The fire is most inviting,
When the air outside is coldest,
The breeze is most refreshing,
When the sun is at its boldest,

The light within the darkness,
Is brightest in the night,
For the world will all take notice,
When you're walking in the light.

The mountain view is greatest,
When you're standing on its peak,
And the world seems much more peaceful,

The eagle finds its glory,
At the apex of its flight,
For you'll see the greatest wonders,
When you're walking in the light.

The river drinks its fullness,
At the mouth that it runs to,
And the bees rush to their honey,
When they taste the morning dew,

The soul longs for its maker,
Bestowed with Holy sight,
For The Lord is your desire,
When you're walking in the light.

The universe awakens,
At the dawning of the day,
The stars renew their sparkle,

As the dark takes light away,

And the brightness of your spirit,
Will glow with Heaven's Might,
For your heart renews its purpose,
When you're walking in the light.

The Little Branch

I started off a little branch that came up from the root,
With tiny little buds on me I hoped would soon be fruit,
I soaked up sunshine, drops of rain, and everything I could,
To grow into a bigger branch the way I knew I should.

But then I found my little buds had somehow failed to flourish,
As I strived against the root that helped me keep my branch well-nourished,
For I sought to be the brightest branch and soar above the rest,
So all the branches in the vine would know that I'm the best.

I'd make the brightest fruit and please the root that I was serving,
I'd branch out more than ere before and be the most deserving,
But still the buds had little growth and nearly lost their beauty,
For all the wonders found in growth I'd sacrificed for duty.

I treated growth as work, and thought I'd earn the root's approval,
Instead, my pride had stunted growth and marked me for removal,
For after all what good am I if I branch out on my own,
When the glory found in every branch is for the root alone?

I asked the dresser of the vine to help me grow once more,
To find again the simple faith I found in Him before,
He pruned me more than I could stand and set me straight again,

Removing all the dying shoots corrupted by my sin.

No longer living for myself, I gave the root control,
Replacing pride with purpose then, He made me fully whole,
And from His guidance fruit emerged, from every blossom grew,
A branch that showed the glory of the root in all I do.

I started off a little branch and now, at last I know,
Abiding humbly in the root is the only way to grow.

The Morning After

It's the morning after,
The rain is all displaced,
The winds have ceased their wailing,
Their bitter hold erased.

It's the morning after,
The pieces are still there,
The broken heart is beating,
In need of gentle care.

It's the morning after,
The ground has drunk its fill,
The cold and bitter water,
Has turned to help you heal.

It's the morning after,
The pieces fit together,
The wounds have found their mending,
For no wound can last forever.

It's the morning after,
The road is dry and clear,
The sun has found its bearings,
The day is finally here.

It's the morning after,
The heart has found its way,
You're stronger for the journey,
In the rising of the day.

The Colors of the Sky

The colors of the sky are the colors of living,
Reflecting their mood in the light they are giving,
Where one is light blue and another bright red,
The hues of the morning, the dark while in bed.

They tell us the sky has a palette of shade,
That tells us a story as colors cascade,
In brightness and darkness, the heavens declare,
The wonder and beauty of all that is fair.

We look to the heart, and we see the same plan,
From the highest and lowest of colors in man,
Despair and regret blend with joy and contentment,
As the heart that holds love often clings to resentment.

Yet all blend in colors as dark turns to light,
With the purples and pinks leading into the night,
While the orange and azure give in to the clearing,
To know that the morning is steadily nearing.

If we lose our perspective in darkening hue,
We find ourselves missing the light of the new,
For more than the black and the white do we find,
That fills up the canvas we keep in our mind.

If God gave us skies that we find so appealing,
Then would he not grant us a rainbow of feeling?
Embraced and in full, we will yet find a way,
To color with beauty our life every day.

The Dawn is There

The dawn is there, creeping just below the dark,
Rising slowly to the surface, anxiously waiting to make its mark,
And there it sits calmly, just beyond your troubled view,
Gently soothing your restless spirit,
Appearing suddenly with the morning dew.

The night is now breaking, both weary and spent,
The stars are all melting, at the start of their descent,
And the star that you wished on, with the dark at its peak,
Makes way for the rising of the brilliance you seek.

The joy you envision, all the things you still ache for,
They are right within reach, in the plans that you wake for,
The future is certain, for the night can't detain,
All the hopes of tomorrow, though it tries to in vain.

For the dawn is here, just beyond the next mount,
With the treasures of promise, too many to count,
Stand fast in its rising, as the darkness gives way,
For the joys of tomorrow are found in today.

Perfect Light

The sun rips through the stinging wind,
Warding off the chill of fall,
As light descends on the bluest skyline,
Breathing life into us all.

For light revives the dreary soul,
With beams of warmth in every place,
Takes hold of dark to cast it off,
And rests its glow upon my face.

How much I've missed your soft refrain,
The silent singing of your glory,
Honeyed sunbeams form a chorus,
Caught up in your timeless story.

Speak to us of God eternal,
Brilliance far beyond our sight,
Show us all the way to Heaven,
Immersed within your perfect light.

The Stinging Cold

The stinging cold is here again,
Its chill is biting deep,
No revelry is found within,
No company to keep.

Mere flesh and bone cannot defend,
Against its icy breath,
For those who brave the frosty wind,
Are courting their own death.

No warmth or heat from the rising sun,
No comfort or respite,
The creeping coldness offers none,
But misery in sight.

But still, we must be in its path,
If progress would be made,
The rain and sleet and icy wrath,
Too common to evade.

For bitter cold and frozen heart,
We've known in seasons past,
And though we wish them all depart,
The cold will never last.

When seasons change, the sun returns,
And bring its heat to bear,
Until that time, there are things to learn,
And warmth enough to share.

The cold and lonely find embrace,
In friendship, love, and laughter,

To warm the soul and light the face,
Before the cold and after.

Take courage heart, in storm and cold,
Find strength in all you do,
In winter's face, be strong, be bold,
And faith will see you through.

The Sun Sets Far Too Quickly

I tried to catch the moment,
But it never seemed to last,
I held onto a snowflake,
But it melted far too fast,

And time slipped through my fingers,
As your face changed overnight,
For the sun sets far too quickly,
When you're standing in the light.

I tried to catch a memory,
To hold on to your years,
But the twinkle in your starlight,
Gave way to evening's tears,

For I can't reverse the process,
And I wouldn't if I could,
For the sun sets far too quickly,
When the sunlight feels so good.

I tried to catch a bluebird,
With wings outstretched and strong,
To recall those days I held you,
When I sang you every song.

But you're grown and sure and steady,
And my work is almost through,
For the sun sets far too quickly,
When I'm holding on to you.

I tried to catch a blossom,
But it bloomed before I could,

Your eyes are filled with knowledge,
Your heart is filled with good,

These moments I will cherish,
Before our days depart,
For the sun sets far too quickly,
When its brightness fills my heart.

In the Dawning of the Day

There is a lazy glow in the wind,
Cascading through the air's embrace,
Illuminating the cool breeze upon my face,
Distilling its luminous display.

There is a hazy glow in the sky,
Tracing pillowy clouds in the broad expanse,
A pattern of beauty too precise for chance,
Welcoming the dawning of the day.

There is a yearning light in the dawn,
Breaking through the endless night,
Bursting forth in radiant light,
As hope turns brighter

There is a burning light in the air,
Pushing through despair and sorrow,
Pressing in through each tomorrow,
Makes my heart lighter,

And hope grows still,
At the dawning of the day.

A Light that Follows Me

There is a light that follows me,
Covers up the lonely places,
In the more secluded spaces,
My thoughts would always find.

There is a fire that swallows me,
Burning all my dried ambition,
Lighting up the cold condition,
Of my weary mind.

There is a moonbeam that hastens me,
Out of my darkened dreariness,
Lifting me out of my weariness,
Into the star-lit sky.

There is a star that has chastened me,
Awaking my soul with intensity,
Challenging every propensity,
Caught in the deep of my eye.

There is a lighthouse that shines for me,
Shines on the course that is right for me,
Guiding my way in the night for me,
Telling me where I should be.

There is a Maker who pines for me,
His brilliance dispels all my fearfulness,
His love brings relief to my tearfulness,
And shine all His glory in me

Section Three: Loss

It's hard to lose people who are a part of you. They never really leave, but their absence puts a hollowness in us that tears at our souls. We think of them and wish so terribly that they were here, but we have a task before us regardless. We must honor those who have left this world so that what they mean to us might be preserved in our memories and in our retelling of their excellent works. More so, we need to put into perspective the eternal promise that those who put their faith in Jesus are not truly dead but only asleep until the Resurrection. We will, if faith holds out, see those who died in Christ. That promise keeps us going and gives us the peace we long for and desperately needed hope. These poems were each written for a particular person who I lost that held meaning to me. One being about a friendship between two Godly women that lasted a lifetime. May you find comfort and peace in these reflections and remember the promise Jesus gives to all who trust in Him.

Forever in our Hearts (Written in Memory of Clarence Lee)

The days seem to expire,
Much quicker than before,
And as we near the ending,
We see it even more.

The moments pass so quickly,
Until our time departs,
But our life is just a moment,
With forever in our hearts.

The world within our memories,
Will never be again,
Though we try to recreate it,
In our minds now and again.

But the past cannot retain us,
When eternal purpose cries,
For we cannot look behind us,
With forever in our eyes.

We mourn the grief we carry,
We miss the friends we lost,
To see them for a moment,
We'd pay a hefty cost.

But their life is far from over,
If in Christ they made their claim,
For the ones who rest in Jesus,
Have forever in their name.

So we look to strength and purpose,
In the promise, we believe,
For the hope we have in glory,
Is a promise we'll receive.

Then as Heaven calls us upward,
And the earth becomes our past,
We will all be reunited,
When forever comes at last.

I know You're Still with Me
(Written in Memory of Dink Autrey)

I know you're still with me, for I know you're still here,
Though your body is absent, your presence is near,
Your spirit rejoices, your tears ever cease,
While you wait for the ending, at rest and in peace.

I know you're still with me, for Heaven's not far,
You're secure at the ready, wherever you are,
Our spirits connected, by love and by grace,
As I long for that moment, to look on your face.

I know you're still with me, for the promise is true,
That we'll all be made perfect when all things are new,
A body eternal, a life that will last,
An end to our hurting and all that has passed.

I know you're still with me, for the time fades away,
Til' we all look together, awaiting that day,
When Jesus will gather His flock one by one,
And we'll see one another when it's all said and done.

I'll know you're still with me, though I wish you were present,
But my thoughts of your smile will make each day more pleasant,
Secure in the knowledge that all will be right,
When the time has expired, when the end is in sight.

I know you're still with me, though my eyes cannot see,
But as God lives within us, you're still here with me,

Eternally bonded, in spirit, in heart,
For I know you're still with me, and you'll never depart.

I Thought I Saw

I thought I saw the rain fall backward,
Ascending on high as it filled the expanse,
And all the things both past and present,
Were frozen in place and refused to advance.

The faces, now gone, came and sat at my table,
Brimming with life and forever made new,
As memories still living within my recalling,
Restored all at once in this wonderful view.

Then those who were present and those who were missing,
Sat down at a table too large to be real,
With laughter and stories that seemed never-ending,
Replacing the loss, I recurrently feel.

We all sat outside on the porch after supper,
And watched as the rain was reversing its spin,
Then I watched with surprise as the ones I'd been missing,
All said their goodbyes and were gone once again.

Yet one took His time as He smiled and nodded,
And I knew as He spoke that the Lord was in sight,
"The rain will ascend once more, my beloved,
And we'll all meet together in glorious flight."

I sat on my porch as I pondered what happened,
The raindrops descending on earth as before,
And I smiled at Heaven for I knew that this moment,
Would come once again and would last evermore.

My Dearest Friend (Written in Memory of Ruby Reed and Her Friendship with Kathryn Turpin)

My dearest friend,
Would you stay for a while and walk with me?
Come my way now if only to talk with me,
Of things we are doing today,

My dearest friend,
Would you laugh at adventures you've shared with me?
Recount all your memories compared with me,
We've collected along the way.

My dearest friend,
Would you smile at the hand you've been dealt with me?
Remember the losses you've felt with me,
Grieving together in tune.

My dearest friend,
Would you share every battle you've fought with me?
Rejoice in each dream you have sought with me,
For the time slips away far too soon.

My dearest friend,
Would you sing a duet to the Lord with me?
Two souls just as one in accord with me,
As we look to the promise above.

My dearest friend,
Would you promise to make your way there with me?
So forever as friends, you can share with me,
The depth of eternity's love.

My dearest friend,
Would you go and prepare a good place for me?
Be there at the end of the race for me,
Cheering me on 'til the end.

My dearest friend,
Would you welcome me there evermore with me?
As you laugh and you talk as before with me,
My truest, my dearest, my friend.

When I'm Thinking Back on You
(Written for Laura Shepherd Upon
the Death of Her Mother)

Your face is still so vivid,
Your voice is clear and bright,
Your eyes retain their color,
In the waning of the light.

Your image holds its substance,
Your scent, your smile, your hue,
For you never really left me,
When I'm thinking back on you.

Your laugh is still contagious,
In the memories I retain,
And in every sweet remembrance,
Your presence will remain.

My loss is only partial,
For I know this to be true,
That you're gone but not forgotten,
When I'm thinking back on you.

The words we spoke together,
Are all pages in my head,
That make up a thousand volumes,
To be cherished when they're read.
Each day I read a chapter,
As the old becomes the new,
For I always gain perspective,
When I'm thinking back on you.

We laughed and cried and cherished,
Every moment we received,
As we found great joy and comfort,
In the things we both believed.

Still, I find a strength and passion,
In the things I say and do,
On the wings of hope and promise,
When I'm thinking back on you.

Now through tears of joy and sorrow,
I still long to see your light,
In the land of full redemption,
When our souls will both take flight.

But until I reach that moment,
I will always make it through,
In the joy of my recalling,
When I'm thinking back on you.

Tears Aren't Forever

Tears of sorrow, tears of pain,
Tears of worry, tears of strain,
Tears of regret, tears of rejection
Tears of the lonely, tears of reflection,

Tears of mourning, tears of the past,
Tears of forgetting, tears that won't last,
Tears that won't stop, tears that won't start,
Tears of the spirit, tears of the heart,

Tears of rejoicing, tears of relief,
Tears of conviction, tears of belief,
Tears of affection, tears of adoring,
Tears that are grateful, tears of outpouring,

Tears of reunion, tears of goodbyes,
Tears held within us, tears in our eyes,
Tears at the ready, tears get us through,
But tears aren't forever when Christ lives in you.

Eternity Calls (In Memory of Jack Cummings)

Eternity calls,
Clarion voice resounding, quiet whisper pounding,
On this aching spirit, the more that I grow near it.

Eternity calls,
Restless soul awaking, newness in the making,
Fills my heart's desire ablaze with holy fire.

Eternity calls,
Dropping all insistence, denying my resistance,
All my will forsaken, the upward path I've taken.

Eternity calls,
Breath of life inhaling, Holy light prevailing,
Darkness torn asunder; voice as loud as thunder.

Eternity calls,
Heaven's gate inviting, loved ones reuniting,
Creation disappearing, Eternity is nearing.

Eternity calls,
The voice of Bride and Spirit, listen if you hear it,
"Come," you souls believing, eternal life receiving.

Eternity calls… Lord, I'm ready.

Section Four: Inspiration

I love being inspired, and I love inspiring others. I've often felt that I was put here on earth to encourage others. I love to preach, teach, talk, and listen, to tell people that they can do so many great things because they are made by a wonderful God. I think we all need inspiration, and poetry is an excellent vessel for that. As we close this poetry book with this last section, my prayer is that if you got anything out of this book, it's that you go forward inspired to be and do more in Christ and that you feel good about the future. We have so much to look forward to in life if we see what life can bring us. Stay strong, stay positive, and be encouraged…It's the most incredible feeling in the world!

A Little Dream

I had a little dream one day,
That spurred me on to act,
I told the people close to me,
To see how they'd react.

They said to me, just try your best,
And give it all you've got,
And so I chased my little dream,
And gave my dream a shot.

I buckled down and sought each day,
To make my dream come true,
And even when I got bogged down,
I'd struggle to push through.

At last, my dream was ready to
Be placed within the world,
And so I spoke my dream aloud,
and let it be unfurled.

And then I faced the troubling task,
Of sharing what I dreamed,
To find someone who saw its worth,
Was harder than it seemed.

Rejection cold and painful played,
Against my will to try,
As time wore out my dreaming heart,
And bled ambition dry.

But still, I held that little dream,
And sought to find its spark,
For the smallest flame grows brighter still,

When everything is dark.

And suddenly the spark took hold,
And then, to my surprise,
The little dream had taken root,
And bloomed before my eyes.

So now I take my little dream,
And never let it go,
For little dreams are far more real,
Than anyone could know.

Everything and Anything

We had nothing and everything,
Everything and anything good and bad,
But it wasn't meant to last.
We all had dreams and desires,
Long nights of wishing and hoping we had,
But it's all in our past.

We had missing teeth and scraped knees,
Awkward years and tender years abundant,
But they were destined to run dry,
Passion, wonder, and unrequited love,
Not a moment ever seemed to be redundant,
But we had to say goodbye.

Youth burned in our hearts so quickly,
Consuming our best and brightest hours,
In a flicker and a spark,
Now we see those days from afar,
And upon us time and distance towers,
Leaving us huddled in the dark.

Yet if we look closely enough,
Everything and anything are not far gone,
The child in us lingers still,
Our passion, our dreams,
Still burn bright and strong within us,
Held fast by the strength of our will,

Youth renewed, restored,
When the child within us awakens,
To restore in us wholeness once more,
We rekindle our flame,

The passing of years has taken,
Stronger, brighter, better...than ever before.

I Tripped and Fell

I tripped and fell the other day,
When I was walking on my way,
To find success and feel complete,
In checking off each goal I meet.

I made a misstep, lost my stride,
And cast my better self aside,
Now here I sit upon the floor,
Wishing I was strong once more.

Reverting happens oh so fast,
To trade the future for the past!
I've gone and stumbled into shame,
With no one else but me to blame.

Then I remember what I gained,
When helpless folly was refrained,
And I was more than I had been,
How has it changed from now to then?

I dusted off my failed attempt,
And knew no soul could be exempt,
From falling short or making an error,
As failing lost its grip of terror.

Boldly standing up once more,
I set my visage as before,
Now wiser in my new approach,
No longer letting doubt encroach.
To try and fail is not the end,
For lessons learned will now descend,
Upon my heart to help me see,
A better way, a better me

In Your Smile

In your smile,
There are a million different reasons,
Far gone days and distant seasons,
Each one of them shines in every grin,
Shows where you are going and where you have been.

In your laugh,
There's a portrait in what I'm seeing,
The joy held deep within your being,
Displaying in a moment all that you're holding,
Your life and your fullness all unfolding.

In your sigh,
A moment of relief and contentment shines through,
The sum of your journey in life echoes through,
The end and beginning of things, new and old,
The cry of the meek and the voice of the bold.

In your tears,
A blend of emotions pours out from your heart,
The sorrow, the joy, each tear might impart,
And in that moment, your soul shows its color,
The highest and lowest, the one or the other.

In your all,
You express every movement of life on your face,
The color of wonder, the texture of grace,
Reflected in fullness, in the place where you stand,
Created and molded by the Master's hand.

Life Makes a Window

Life makes a window for every wall,
And a doorway for every wrong turn,
A diamond in coal, fine linen from flax,
And mistakes mark the lessons we learn,

Life pours out our faults and lays hammer to heart,
Spinning gold out of changes we thread,
When our normal is lost, and we've counted our cost,
We find fortune when we're far in the red.

Life clears our vision when chaos abounds,
When derailed from our usual pace,
For the valleys, we find, at the foot of our climb,
Holds a beauty we rarely embrace.

Life steals our comfort with hardship's hand,
Robbing ease of its dampening flow,
Till acquainted with tears and well-versed in our fears,
We grow strong in adversity's throe.

Life makes a puzzle of what seems complete,
Begs faith when our wisdom has failed,
So when Life gives us pause, no matter the cause,
Pay attention so that Life might prevail.

Lonely Street Lamp

You barely shine away the dark,
In this cold of mid-October,
Your metal frame resists the winds,
As a guard, both strong and sober.

Yet for the wandering souls that stir,
You offer some refrain,
Against the bitter dark of fall,
So eyes might cease to strain,

How brief your time of hazy glow,
How small a scene you paint,
Yet there is beauty in your wake,
Though bound by deep constraint.

How much I feel your mellow hues,
And know your lonely work,
To glow in looming shadows long,
And never from them shirk.

Yet as my eyes are raised afar,
There's comfort in the view,
For lonely lamps raised in the dark,
Are keeping watch with you.

They cast their light upon the trail,
Cascading down the way,
To offer up a hope, a dream,
At the dawning of the day.

More Beautiful

Did you know you're more beautiful than the day that I met you?
For your soul shines much brighter, the more that I get you,
As I learn every facet of your passion and strength,
For to those whom you live for, you'll go any length.

Did you know you're more beautiful, as you take it in stride?
For the pain in your struggle is too great to hide,
Yet you never quit going, as you reach for your goal,
While you pull in the broken to make yourself whole.

Did you know you're more beautiful the older you get?
For the One who has shaped you is not finished yet,
His hands are perfecting, the visage within,
And the look you are given, He's improving again.

Did you know you're more beautiful, as your kindness has grown you?
For your love has grown deeper, the longer I've known you,
Your eyes full of wisdom, from long days of learning,
Your heart full of Jesus, for whom you are yearning.

Did you know you're more beautiful, my dear and true friend?
For the growth in your beauty has not met its end,
There is no fading glory, In a heart full of love,
For the well of your beauty is fed from above.

Reflection

Reflection, I said, it's been a while,
Since I saw you laugh or even smile,
At some small thing, we both found funny,
To make our disposition sunny,

Reflection, I said, you've said some things,
That only dark reflection brings,
About how bad it's been of late,
Or bad enough at any rate,

Reflection, I said, we've had some days,
Where we almost thought of parting ways,
Afraid to mirror what you would see,
When you saw the darkest part of me,

Reflection, I said, we've been through worse,
We've talked this out and can't reverse,
The battles we have fought within,
To make our peace and start again.

Reflection, I said, pray words of peace,
Let joy return and darkness cease,
To dim the beauty in your eyes,
Or mask the truth in shallow lies.

Reflection, I said, we might be broken,
But hope remains when words are spoken,
Child of light, forgiven still,
Reflected in the Father's will,

Reflection, I said, within your face,
I look upon the Savior's grace,

From glory dim to brilliance gleaming,
With eyes attuned to love redeeming.

Reflection, I said, we'll be okay,
Lift up your head and start your day,
Let storm and shadow fade from view,
And rejoice with me in all we do.

The Choice

There's no dark within us unless we make it,
There's nothing that's broken unless we break it,
There's nothing to tempt us except for desire,
There's nothing to burn us except our own fire.

There's not an excuse devoid of a choice,
There's not a word spoken beyond our own voice,
There's never an action we take past our knowing,
There's never a path we take without going.

There's nothing to hope for if hope is neglected,
There's nothing to live for if life is rejected,
There's no room for love if your heart has been shuttered,
There's no room for God if your prayers are not uttered.

The things that we do and the things we say,
The way that we work and the way that we play,
We choose our own life for the good or the ill,
To live for yourself or to live for God's will.

The choice is for you, and no other can make it,
So make a good choice while you're able to take it.

How Do You Sing? (For My Mother)

How do you sing? Said the sparrow to me,
Who taught you to whistle? Who taught you to see,
Where the wonders around you were hiding away,
In the cool of the evening, in the warmth of the day?

How do you shine? Said the sun far above,
Who taught you to laugh? Who taught you to love?
In a time long forgotten and in all that was said,
Who taught you to smile at the days still ahead?

How do you grow? Said the grass at my feet,
Who taught you to walk? Who taught you to eat?
Who taught you to listen, be thoughtful and speak,
With kindness and patience, to be gentle and meek?

How do you weep? Said the tears in my eye,
Who taught you to mourn? Who taught you to cry?
When the words would not come, and your heart was in pain,
Who showed you the rainbow at the end of the rain?

How do you bloom? Said the flowers in May,
Who taught you to trust? Who taught you to pray?
When your faith was poured into the shape of your soul,
Who told you that God was the one in control?

How do I bloom? How do I sing?
How do I know how to do anything?
Who but a mother could teach what I know,
To weep and laugh, to shine and to grow?

How did you do it? Said the child in me,
How did you help make me all I could be?
All I can give you is praise that is due,
And to thank God in Heaven for giving me you.

No One Stopped Me

No-one stopped me from waking up,
From breaking ground on morning's start,
From the sun's first rise to the star's descent,
None but the echoes in my own heart.

No-one stopped me from trying hard,
Against the tides of life's resistance,
Or held me back from any work,
Unless it's from my own insistence.

No-one stopped me from chasing dreams,
Or seeking all my soul might treasure,
No force defies where I aspire,
Unless it comes from my own measure.

No-one stopped me from seeking life,
Or told me faith was not required,
No wicked plot destroyed my hope,
Except for all my flesh desired.

No-one stopped me, and no one can,
For I resign my stubborn way,
Embracing all that life can give,
I'm ready now to start my day.

www.ingramcontent.com/pod-product-compliance
Lightning Source LLC
Chambersburg PA
CBHW030915080526
44589CB00010B/309